2001 RAOUL WALLENBERG LECTURE

Published to commemorate the Raoul Wallenberg Lecture,
given by Rafael Moneo at the College on April 13th, 2001.

Editors: Brian Carter and Annette W. LeCuyer
Design: Christian Unverzagt with Craig Somers at M1, Detroit
Typeset in Monotype Baskerville and Monotype Grotesque
Printed and bound in the United States of America
ISBN: 1-891197-15-0

Taubman College
2000 Bonisteel Boulevard, Ann Arbor, Michigan 48109-2069 USA

734 764 1300
734 763 2322 fax
www.tcaup.umich.edu

THE FREEDOM OF THE ARCHITECT

RAFAEL MONEO

FOREWORD

Raoul Gustaf Wallenberg was born in Stockholm in 1912. He was a member of one of Sweden's most distinguished families who, under the guidance and patronage of his grandfather, enrolled as a student at the University of Michigan in 1931.

Raoul Wallenberg studied architecture and graduated from the University of Michigan with honors in 1935, when he also received the American Institute of Architects' Silver Medal. His training, tenacity and organizational skills were to prove invaluable. Returning to Europe, he became increasingly aware of the plight of Jews, Gypsies, communists, homosexuals and those not of Nazi persuasion. Soon after Hitler had ordered Adolf Eichmann to prepare for the annihilation of the Jewish population in Hungary, Raoul Wallenberg went to Budapest to serve as first secretary of the Swedish delegation. During the months that followed, he moved quickly to save the lives of more than 100,000 people who would otherwise almost certainly have perished. Combining insight, intelligence and unbelievable courage, he issued fake passports and set up safe houses; created hospitals, soup kitchens and shelters; bribed German officials with money from the United States War Refugee Fund; and threatened others with war crimes trials after the war. In an extraordinary series

of individual acts of courage, he repeatedly put his own
life at risk in order to save others.

When the Russians surrounded Budapest in
December 1944, the end of World War II was in sight
and on 17 January 1945, Wallenberg and his driver
went to meet the Russian Commander. They were
never seen again.

To honor this outstanding alumnus, and one
of the twentieth century's most significant heroes, the
Raoul Wallenberg Lecture was initiated in 1971 by
Sol King, one of Wallenberg's former classmates. Five
years later, an endowment was established to present
an annual lecture focused on architecture as a humane
and social art. It is a lecture which honors Wallenberg's
legendary acts of compassion and bravery and recognizes the power of an individual to make a difference.
It also serves to remind us that as architects, and as
members of the community of human beings, our lives
and our work have a critical ethical dimension.

The first Raoul Wallenberg Lecture was given at
the College in 1972 by Sir Nikolaus Pevsner. Others
have subsequently been given by Rudolf Arnheim,
Reyner Banham, Charles Correa, Denise Scott Brown,
Daniel Libeskind and most recently by Michael Benedikt.
It is a great honor for the College and for the University
of Michigan to host this important annual event.

Brian Carter,
Professor of Architecture

INTRODUCTION

When he was saving lives in Budapest, one of the things that must have made life more difficult and risky for Raoul Wallenberg was language. He was coaching, negotiating, wheedling, cajoling, pleading, and obfuscating in Hungarian, German, Yiddish and who knows what other tongues foreign to his native Swedish.

Let me offer a few words about language and architecture as part of this introduction to Rafael Moneo, who often must also communicate in a second language. I refer especially to written language, not so much the language of transaction and agency that preoccupied Raoul Wallenberg, but more the language of expression.

English is perhaps the most supple of languages, offering the most combinatorial possibilities and the richest assortment of words, or at least the greatest number of them with which to work. It is also relatively economical, which is easily calibrated when English text is run side by side with, say, French text in a multi-lingual magazine or exhibit.

This combinatorial articulation is also true of English high-tech buildings designed by architects like Foster, Rogers, and Grimshaw. These light but muscular buildings are suggestive of strong, masculine nouns, with lots of articles, prepositions and conjunctions to hold them together. These bold structures have precise metal joints and elegant details that are tectonically and visually refined.

Spanish, Rafael Moneo's native language, is more rational than English. There are fewer words, which are more consistently deployed in more predictable syntax, with fewer exceptions to the rules. In short, Spanish is more typological. It is typological because it is not as loose, quotidian or idiosyncratic as English. It has stricter and more consistent grammar – a Latinate clarity rather than a cobbled richness. Professor Moneo wrote a seminal essay on typology in 1978, which noted Modernism's outright rejection of typological precedent in its headlong search for new forms and tectonics. It is still cited often in academia, as schools of architecture have continued to struggle with the central dialectic of typology – precedent versus innovation.

It is important to point out that Rafael Moneo is a writer, an academic, and a practitioner. He has done honor to all three professions – and for a long time. I remember inviting and introducing him at the second International Daylighting Conference in California two decades ago. His buildings were better considered than buildings by his American peers in their relationship to the warmth and light of the sun. The sun is of course stronger and insists on more attention in a Mediterranean climate and culture than in northern Europe or here in Michigan. But Rafael Moneo has also done exemplary work in Stockholm, which is about as far north as Architecture with a capital "A" happens and about as inhospitable a climate as a city gets. He has designed a handsome and understated new art museum there, and he is building in American cities – Houston and Los Angeles among others.

His new art facility at Cranbrook is designed in a Modernist vocabulary, but honors a traditional master plan without trying to re-invent the architecture and urbanism of the campus. His *parti* is based on familiar architectural types and is not about starting over on this extraordinary American campus, or most contexts in which he is asked to work. A typological, historical, contextual and climatological understanding informs Moneo's work. It is inventive but not for the sake of invention, nor is it slavishly historical, contextual or environmental.

Rafael Moneo's architecture is urbanistically considered and considerate, unlike much of the work of many contemporary American star architects. True to his linguistic and cultural roots, his urbane work adds to but does not dominate its surroundings. It tends toward the mature and tolerant, rather than the audacious and self-centered. The work is morphologically and materially sensitive to the city, without being simple-minded or scenographic.

There also is a certain gravitas about Moneo's buildings. They have the solidity, rhythm and finitude – without being predictable or boring – that good cityscapes need, despite post-structuralist protestations to the contrary. His antiquities museum in Merida and the handsome town hall at Murcia have a sense of palpable weight and permanence. There is a freshness and ambiguity to the town hall façade – a digital, almost random trabeation, but with a stately monumentality. The ambiguity stems from the fact that the front façade is cropped with no cornice to cap the expected classical composition of base, middle, and top. The stateliness arises from the siting and building materials used.

Moneo's language is sophisticated but visually simple and tectonically fundamentalist. There are no gymnastics or pyrotechnics here. His buildings will weather well and be easy to maintain. They are the kind of buildings that build civic affection. They will endure physically and culturally, which is why many of Rafael Moneo's buildings have become modern classics. There are surely more to come.

We hope this modest book and the architecture it presents will add to Rafael Moneo's well-deserved honor and reputation, while perpetuating – in the written word of their second language – the memory of Raoul Wallenberg.

Douglas S. Kelbaugh FAIA,
Dean

THE FREEDOM OF THE ARCHITECT

I am touched when thinking about why we have come together here and now. To honor the memory of someone like Raoul Wallenberg is an important endeavor. We architects are proud of him and of his courage and righteous behavior in such difficult circumstances. He is an admirable example of a person endowed with the most valuable virtues; the portrait we have of him projects compassion and talent. He wanted to be an architect. Unfortunately, he did not fulfill his calling, but he has left all of us a spiritual legacy more valuable than any architectural work.

I am therefore honored when considering that we are celebrating his memory with a presentation of my work. To begin, I would like to reflect upon the problems faced by architects today:

If architects, having lost the interest in an architecture maintaining continuity with the past and ignoring the figurative goals of today, are looking for a direct and authoritative representation of today's world, what are the issues attracting them? How do they intend to reflect the world around us? Architects are concerned with capturing the mobility and the fleeting, unstable condition of a world that seems to resist the idea of any fixed image. Form, something always associated with architecture, is seen now as something static, something that, because it endures, has little to do with today's fluid culture. Today, our world is conveyed mostly by electronic screens, witnesses to a world changing at every instant, belying stability. Waves express this representation of form over time. Waves, apparently camouflaged, blend with the landscape, trying to avoid any sense of consolidation. Architecture should be able to reflect this mobile condition of the world around us. Reality presents itself as fragmented and broken, discontinuous and incomprehensible. Architecture in the past sought the opposite. The architecture we received from the past seemed to long for an identity where buildings possessed their own autonomy and independence. But the model which scientific knowledge offers today suggests the opposite: a world interconnected yet discontinuous and diverse, multiple and fragmented.

So without shared values, without any clear expectations of architecture, with the easy application of sophisticated technical tools, and with the awareness that the old city is gone, architects no longer believe in an architecture founded on disciplinary principles inspired by other works in the visual arts. Architects do not believe that today's world is represented either by artistic trends or by a common figurative language that might give form to a universal culture. Without such help, eager to participate in the extremely active and energetic world of today, architects immerse themselves in the search for an architecture able to re-establish links with the world around. Architects once again are urgently seeking the spirit of the time, the "zeitgeist." I believe that is where we are today in architecture.

Many questions are raised by this ingenuous way of representing today's visual atmosphere. The very first would be to question whether or not this "direct realism" – such as waves embodying unstable forms – is a legitimate way to represent the current world. I wonder whether our contemporary condition could be expressed more naturally in a less contrived way.

Now that the earlier desire for a universal language is gone, individuals prevail in the architecture of today. As a consequence, either the architecture is tempted by the ambition of becoming a work of art, or falls directly into anarchy. Abandoned is the fantasy of a new architecture as nature's replica; forgotten is any temptation – very present in modern architecture – of an organic architecture still inspired by an Aristotelian cosmology. Today architects enter into the domain of the personal. Therefore, it is no longer possible to speak about schools or about styles. Instead we talk about individuals.

What will the issues be in the near future? I want to insist on the fact that architecture is not dictated solely by different local conditions. We should admit that it is the prerogative of the architect to choose the formal conventions with which to build. That implies reflection and some theoretical commitments. One should ask generic questions, such as, what is the appropriate continuity with the built surroundings? – questions that immediately emphasize the importance of a shared language that might overcome the wild individualism of today. In other words, it leads us to consider those specific features that define this activity called architecture. I realize that to insist on this point could sound odd just now, but I am compelled to remind you about the relevance of explicit theoretical conditions of this so much beloved activity called architecture.

The projects presented here attempt to give an answer to the question raised in the previous paragraphs. I am not mechanically representing the world around me. I am trying to make an architecture that recognizes the freedom of the architect to make choices that bring with them the consolidation of form implicit in any construction. These choices must be inspired, but not dictated by circumstances or by the ideology of the architect, who – and I want to emphasize this point – acts with a certain degree of freedom when dealing with the materials offered by the received heritage of architectural knowledge.

The City Hall of Murcia

The new building for the City Hall of Murcia literally fills a void and this, without a doubt, helps the Cardinal Belluga Plaza regain its character. The plaza embodies the celebratory spirit of the baroque, and the new building is content in its role as a spectator, not seeking the status of protagonist held by the Cathedral and the Cardinal Belluga Palace. It is not, however, a commonplace spectator. Civil power is embodied in this new building on the plaza. In this space imbued with the importance of the Church and the power that proceeded from it in the 18th century, the building represents the authority of the citizens, the City Government of Murcia. In this way an old conflict is resolved. Until now the City Hall of Murcia, placed on the river, had ignored the plaza, perhaps the city's most important urban space.

All of this was translated into architectural terms with the design of a façade which takes the form of a *retablo* facing the Cathedral. Now the city government is able to take part in the life of the plaza; it can participate in public events such as processions, which are enhanced by the splendid backdrop of the Cathedral's facade. However, it is important to note that the City Hall annex does not have an entrance on the plaza. The building is located on the plaza but respects the pre-eminence of those buildings that have occupied it for so long. For this reason, the entrance door was placed on one of its flanks on Frenerá Street, literally making an end to Polo

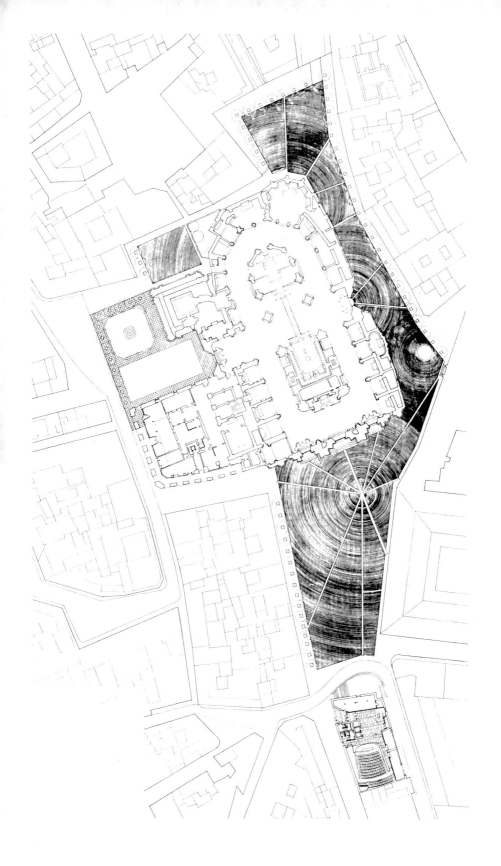

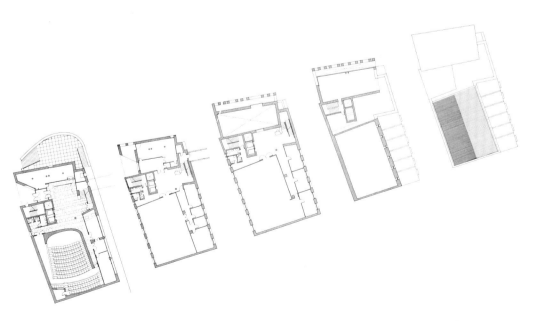

Medina Street. In this way, the continuity between the city and the City Hall is established with the entrance allowing the City Hall to be reached directly from the historic center.

The new *retablo* facing the plaza could never, nor would ever, want to compete with this classical order. It is organized as a musical score, numerically, accepting the system of horizontal levels of the floor slabs. The façade resists symmetries and offers as its key element the balcony of the gallery. The balcony of the City Hall annex is at the same height as the central balcony of the piano nobile of Cardinal Belluga Palace. The façade of the new building is oriented towards the Cathedral. The four sides of the plaza are independent, enabling each of the buildings around the plaza to preserve its autonomy. The new building floats without establishing any orthogonal relationship with the existing buildings, deferring only to the façade of the Cathedral despite the distance between them. In this way, the corner of the current City Hall is freed up and the visual relationship between Frenerá and San Patricio Streets is established. The lateral façades, more discreet and with modest openings, are adapted to the dimensions of the side streets.

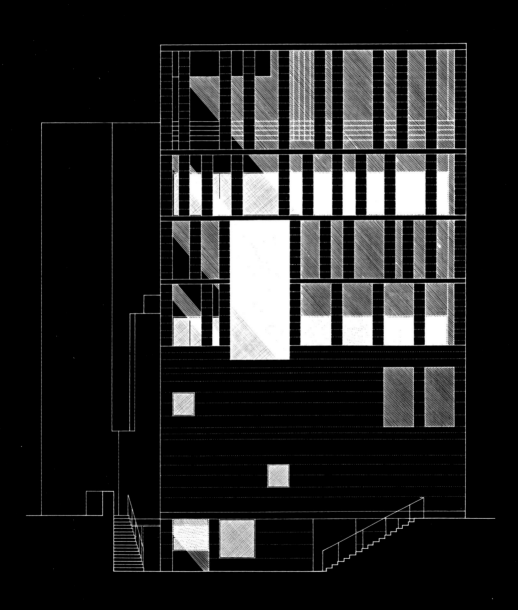

The Museum of Fine Arts of Houston

The Museum of Fine Arts of Houston was built in 1924, following the design of the architect William Ward Watkin. Much later, Mies van der Rohe built extensions, first in 1958 and again in 1974. It is enough to say that the architecture of Mies has prevailed and today the modest and dignified architecture of the first museum has been absorbed in the severe and dark metal framework of the German master.

A new building for the Museum, the Audrey Jones Beck Building, provides additional exhibit spaces for the collections and is joined to the original museum by an underground exhibition gallery and passage. However, the new building cannot be considered an extension in the most literal sense of the word. Located on Main Street – the street that connects the downtown with the Medical Center – the Audrey Jones Beck Building is a separate and autonomous building. The new Museum occupies a rectangular parcel defined by Main Street, Fannin Street, Binz Avenue and Ewing Avenue. In spite of the apparent homogeneity of the street grid, study of the neighborhood soon made me appreciate certain characteristics of the site. The orientation of the new building was the first design decision. The Audrey Jones Beck Building opens onto Main Street, making it the dominant orientation. Main Street is a street of crucial importance in the city. In placing the principal façade on this street, homage is paid to the museum of Mies van der Rohe and a relationship is established that is absolutely necessary.

However, having made such an assertion, it must be said that, in Houston, buildings are perceived from the automobile. This makes it difficult to apply the same criteria as when considering buildings as objects with a well-defined image. In Houston, the frontal view of a building experienced by pedestrians is not possible. Such considerations led the Audrey Jones Beck Building to occupy practically all of the land available, without falling into the temptation of artificial fragmentation. The site provided the opportunity to explore the potential of a compact architecture built within tight confines. It is always desirable to enclose the largest possible volume in the smallest possible surface area. Compact architecture clearly shows how it is possible to break down a regular surface into a whole series of figures that define rooms and corridors, stairs and openings, galleries and light courts, endowing the space with admirable continuity and contiguity without submitting to a pre-established *parti*. Compact architecture gives rise to saturated, dense floor plans that make use of the interstitial spaces to encourage movement, and it can permit surprising liberty in the disposition of architectural programs.

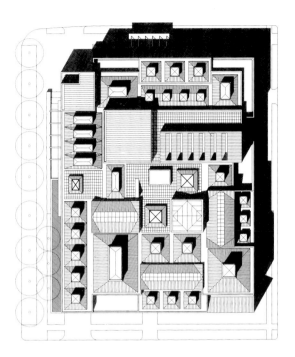

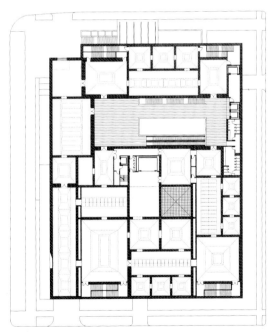

The Museum of Fine Arts is a clear example of
this way of understanding architecture. The floor plan
of the museum is "broken" into a series of rooms and
galleries connected by means of a hidden path that,
without being imperious, guides the visitor's steps. The
museum makes intense use of natural light that illuminates
the rooms and galleries from above. The variety of
the galleries is reflected in the fragmented and broken
outline of a roof that becomes the most characteristic
image of the museum showing the importance given
to light, the real protagonist of an architecture whose
substance is found in the interior space.

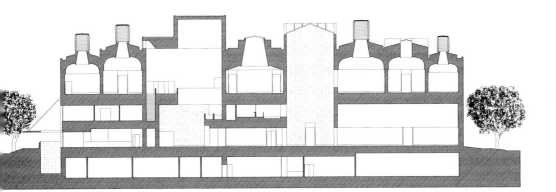

The Kursaal Auditorium and Congress Center

The beauty of San Sebastian is largely due to its environment, to its landscape. Few cities are endowed with more favorable natural conditions. The Concha beach interrupts the Cantabrian Sea, producing in this reduced stretch of coastline all known geographic accidents: bays, islands, beaches, estuaries, and mountains. And connecting all of them is San Sebastian, a city that throughout its history has known how to respect the geography in which it lies.

The site of the Kursaal is a geographic accident, and our response to it was to propose a building that would not violate the presence of the river in the city. The Auditorium and the Congress Hall, the key programmatic elements of the scheme, are conceived as separate autonomous volumes, as two gigantic rocks stranded at the mouth of the river, forming part of the landscape rather than belonging to the city. The exhibition halls, meeting rooms, offices, a restaurant, and musicians' services are contained in the platform that provides a suitable base for the cubic masses of the Auditorium and Congress Hall.

The Auditorium contained within the larger of the two prismatic volumes measures approximately 65 x 46 x 22 meters and celebrates its character of quasi-geographical accident with a slight inclination towards the sea. The volume of the 1,806-seat auditorium is inscribed asymmetrically inside the glass prism, seeming to float within it. The asymmetry is oriented in such a

way that a visitor entering the foyer is unconsciously led towards the highest level, where Mount Urgull and the sea in all of its splendor can be contemplated from a single window. This window punctures the building's double wall, composed of a steel frame clad inside and out with special laminated glass panels. The result is a neutral and luminous interior space. The only contact with the outside world is through the foyer window. Outside, the glass surfaces protect against salt-laden winds from the sea, making the volume a dense, opaque, yet changing mass by day, and a mysterious and dazzling source of light by night.

The rectangular hall adheres to the formula deemed best by acoustical technicians, with a nearly square plan, a flat ceiling and a volume of approximately ten cubic meters per spectator. The continuity and freestanding condition of the hall should be noticed, since patrons can reach all areas from any of the doors.

Similar design and structural criteria have been used in planning the smaller Congress Hall, which is also inscribed in an inclined prism measuring 43 x 32 x 20 meters. The asymmetry here is less evident, but the view from the foyer of Mount Ulá and the sea in the background are just as spectacular.

In the open space of the plinth are found access stairs to the 500-car garage, information and ticket booths, and the entrances to the Auditorium and Congress Hall.

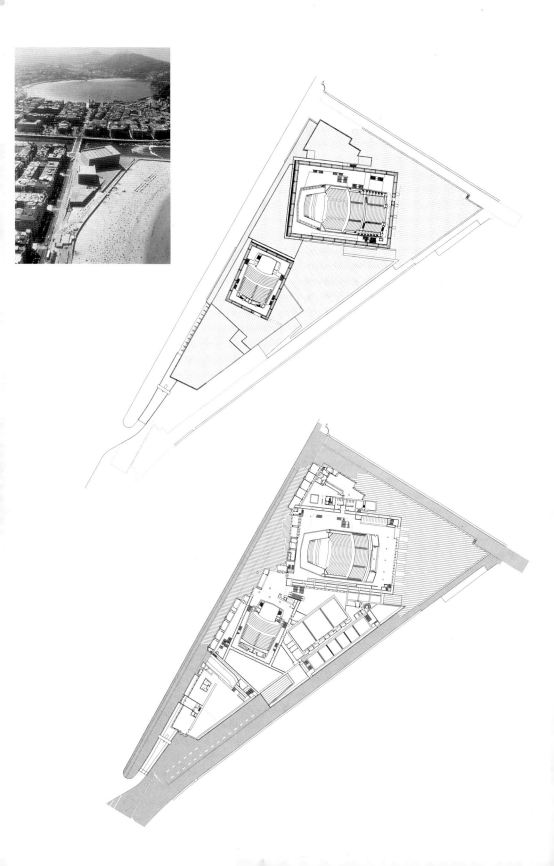

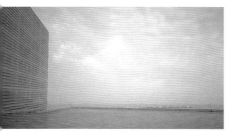

This platform serves as the meeting space between the cultural center and the city, opening onto the Avenue de la Zurriola and providing a wide outdoor space for public access. In this manner, the new cultural center is intended to be a significant urban episode in what has always been a breathtakingly beautiful stretch between Mount Ulá and Mount Igueldo.

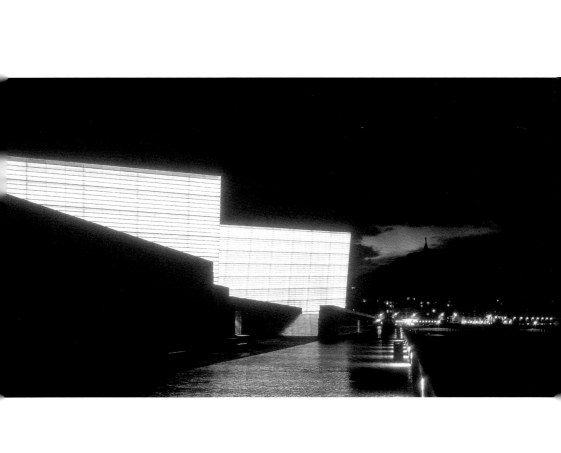

Our Lady of the Angels Cathedral

When I began to think about the Cathedral, I tried to recall in which modern architectures the presence of the sacred could be felt. The church in Turku by Erik Bryggmann and the chapel at Ronchamp by Le Corbusier came to mind. They are the two contemporary churches that have impressed me the most, and I would say they both share the importance of light. I understand light as the protagonist of a space that tries to recover the sense of the 'transcendent.' It is the vehicle through which we are able to experience what we call sacred.

Light is the origin of the Cathedral of Our Lady of the Angels. On the one hand, the light captured by the large windows and reflected from the chapels orients us along the path of the ambulatories that takes us to the nave. This light is not very different from that found in Romanesque churches. On the other hand, the light filtered through the alabaster creates a luminous, diffuse and enveloping atmosphere in which the constructed elements float, ensuring a spatial experience close to that of various Byzantine churches. Finally, the glass cross which presides over the apse lets us understand light as a mystic metaphor of the presence of God. This presence is manifested in the rays of sunlight that come through the cross, bringing about an architectural experience similar to those achieved by architects of the Baroque.

The site for the new Cathedral is in the heart of the city tangent to the Hollywood Freeway, one of the major arteries of the metropolis. Slightly elevated, the

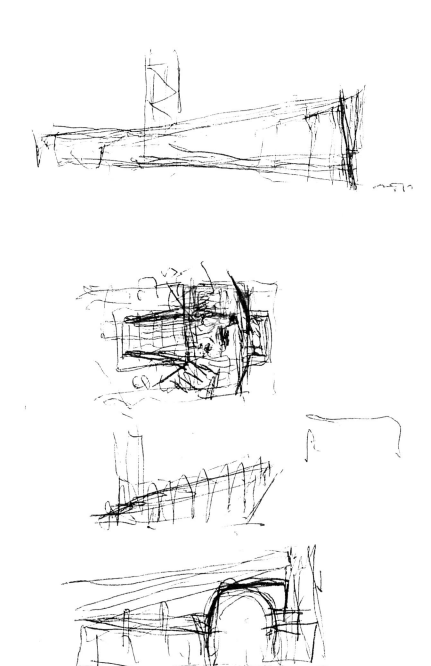

L.H. 13.9.96

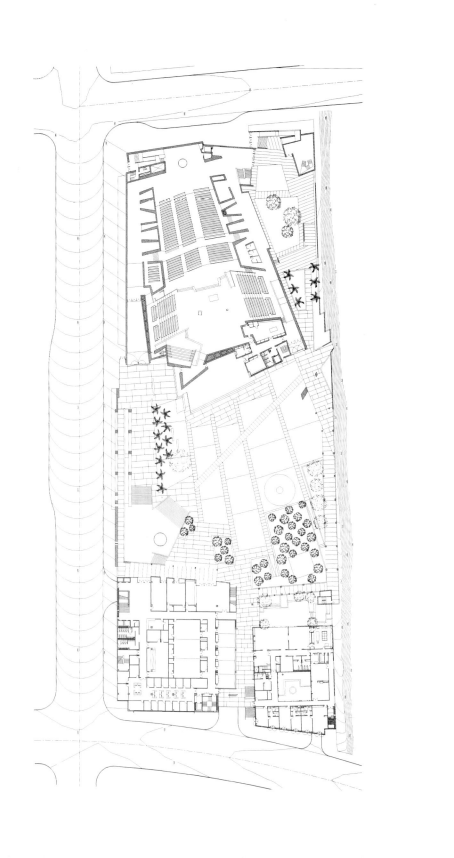

parcel dominates its surroundings, emphasizing the role of the Cathedral as an urban landmark and a spiritual center. An esplanade for large congregations of up to 6,000 people takes up the center of the site with the built volumes at either end connected by colonnades that define the edges of the plaza. The Cathedral occupies the higher end, its front facade at a slight angle with the long axis of the site. The bell tower rises at the corner, set apart from the church by a trapezoidal cloister projecting into the esplanade in the form of a triangular pond bordered by palm trees. At the opposite end of the site are the bishop's residence and facilities for the archdiocese, two volumes that defer to the sculptural mass of the temple. The visual focus of the exterior space is the Franciscan cross cut into the alabaster skylight of the Cathedral facade. The transverse band of the cross is placed in line with the edge of the roof that juts out like a visor. This forward projection of the roof and its perpendicular drop on one side turns the main façade of the Cathedral into a backdrop for open-air ceremonies. The same cross presides over both indoor and outdoor altars.

One enters the Cathedral directly from the esplanade through side doors into a perimeter corridor separated from the space of the nave by outward facing

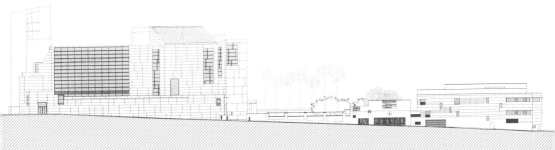

side chapels. This results in a less cluttered central space and allows several religious events to take place simultaneously. The Temple Street door provides access to a gallery that receives reflected light from the chapels. The long outer wall is without windows, so that it can be used for the stone plaques, inscriptions and votive offerings that will keep the history of the Cathedral alive. Between the chapels, one can discern the space of the nave. To the west, opposite the presbytery, is the baptismal font. One can step out onto Grand Street or the cloister directly from the baptistry. The corridor on the north side assumes a different character with the chapels looking out into the cloister garden, bringing them in contact with nature and the landscape of Los Angeles beyond.

The nave – with a capacity for 2,000 worshippers – and the main altar and attendant pulpit flanked by tiers of seating occupy the central longitudinal band of the Cathedral. A large window with a cross dominates the altar and the religious connotations of light are reinforced by the slant of its projecting planes. The choir is placed beside the altar, pushed to the rear of the chancel in an open box, above which rises the organ. The façade surfaces behind the organ consist of alabaster louvers which create a second focus of diffused light in the altar area. The same method of filtered illumination is used for the large windows of the nave's lateral façade.

I hope that my comments about the architect's commitment to choices that imply freedom can be appreciated through these four projects. I feel fully responsible for the choice of the *retablo* as an answer to the civic atmosphere of the plaza in Murcia. Nobody forced me. There were no circumstances dictating that the building façade should take the form of a *retablo*. Similarly, I believe that occupying the entire site in Houston was the right strategy in developing the museum's program, and that the succession of disparate galleries filling up the entire plan helps to effectively display a collection characterized by diversity. There was no one telling me that I should take this approach, one that I recognize as an insightful architectural perception, a response to a specific problem. Indeed, I like to explain the Kursaal project in San Sebastian as the result of my reaction to the landscape. But it should be said that it was the architect who gave prominence to the nature of the site when contemplating an Auditorium and Congress Center.

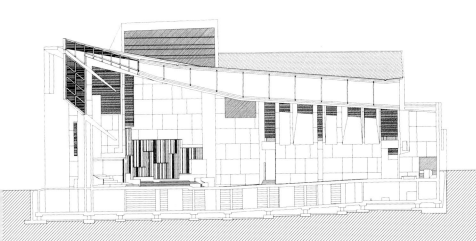

Finally, during my struggle to update an architecture committed to the sacred, I started from a clear understanding of the urban design conditions of the site. I therefore knew where the Cathedral, the plaza, the residence, social center and the parking garage should be, but I did not know the architectural character of the space that was to be called sacred. I let myself reflect on my experiences of sacred spaces and I made my own free selection among my own earlier buildings, drawing from those that seemed to be closest to such an experience. In the end, I chose the atmosphere of the Miró Foundation in Palma de Mallorca as the frame of reference for the architecture that was to become the new Cathedral.

Why all of this reflection? Because I would like to emphasize that even though some architects would like to see their work understood as the result of a deterministic approach to architecture, it is my feeling that just the opposite occurs, that architecture begins as the free choice of the architect. In the presentation of these four projects I want to manifest something I firmly believe, that freedom prevails in the architect's work in spite of all the mediations and that the fantasy of an architecture dictated only by circumstances, an architecture based in mere determinism, should be forgotten.

Rafael Moneo

RAOUL WALLENBERG LECTURE

The Raoul Wallenberg Lecture was initiated in 1971 by Sol King, a former classmate of Wallenberg's. An endowment was established in 1976 for an annual lecture to be offered in Raoul's honor on the theme of architecture as a humane social art. The following distinguished architects and historians have been invited to present the Wallenberg Lectures to the A. Alfred Taubman College of Architecture and Urban Planning at the University of Michigan:

1972	Sir Nikolaus Pevsner	1990	Elizabeth Hollander
1973	Eric Larabee	1991	Joseph Esherick
1975	Reyner Banham	1992	Denise Scott Brown
1976	Rudolf Arnheim	1993	James Ingo Freed
1978	Jacob B. Bakema	1994	Jorge Silvetti
1979	James Marston Fitch	1995	Daniel Libeskind
1981	Carl Levin	1996	Vincent Scully
1983	Edmund Bacon	1997	Michael Sorkin
1984	Charles Correa	1998	Richard Sennett
1985	Grady Clay	1999	Kenneth Frampton
1986	Joseph Rykwert	2000	Michael Benedikt
1987	Spiro Kostof	2001	Rafael Moneo
1989	J. Max Bond, Jr.		

RAOUL WALLENBERG SCHOLARSHIP

The Raoul Wallenberg Scholarship is awarded through a design competition which is held annually for undergraduates in their final year of study in the University of Michigan Architecture Program. The following students have been awarded the scholarship:

1988   John DeGraaf
1989   Matthew Petrie
1990   Elizabeth Govan
1991   Paul Warner
1992   Dallas Felder
1993   Eric Romano
1994   Charles Yoo
1995   Matthew Johnson
1996   Jo Polowczuk
1997   Joseph Rom
1998   Michael Lee
1999   Adam Clous
2000   Lina Lee/Jonathan M. Dickson
2001   Christopher Johnston

ACKNOWLEDGMENTS

The A. Alfred Taubman College of Architecture and Urban Planning is grateful for the generous support for the Raoul Wallenberg Scholarship and Lecture which has been provided by alumni and friends, and by the Bernard L. Maas Foundation.

Rafael Moneo's comments on pp.12-15 are from his presentation at the *ANY Conference* in June 2000.

The College would like to thank Rafael Moneo for the time and energy which he has given to make this publication possible. The photographs and drawings have been published courtesy of Rafael Moneo. We also wish to acknowledge the assistance of the staff working in his office in Madrid, with special thanks to Sandra Rush, who has been an invaluable help.

Photography Credits
© Aker/Zvonkovic: 26. © Aurofoto: 42.
© David Cardelus: 36. F.O.A.T.: 30, 34.
Juan de Dios Hernández: 38. Hester & Hardaway: 24.
Roland Holbe: 33a. Mulstead: 28.
Duccio Malagamba: 16, 19, 23, 32, 33b, 35, 37.
Megías: 20. Michigan Alumnus: 4. Grant Mudford: 43.